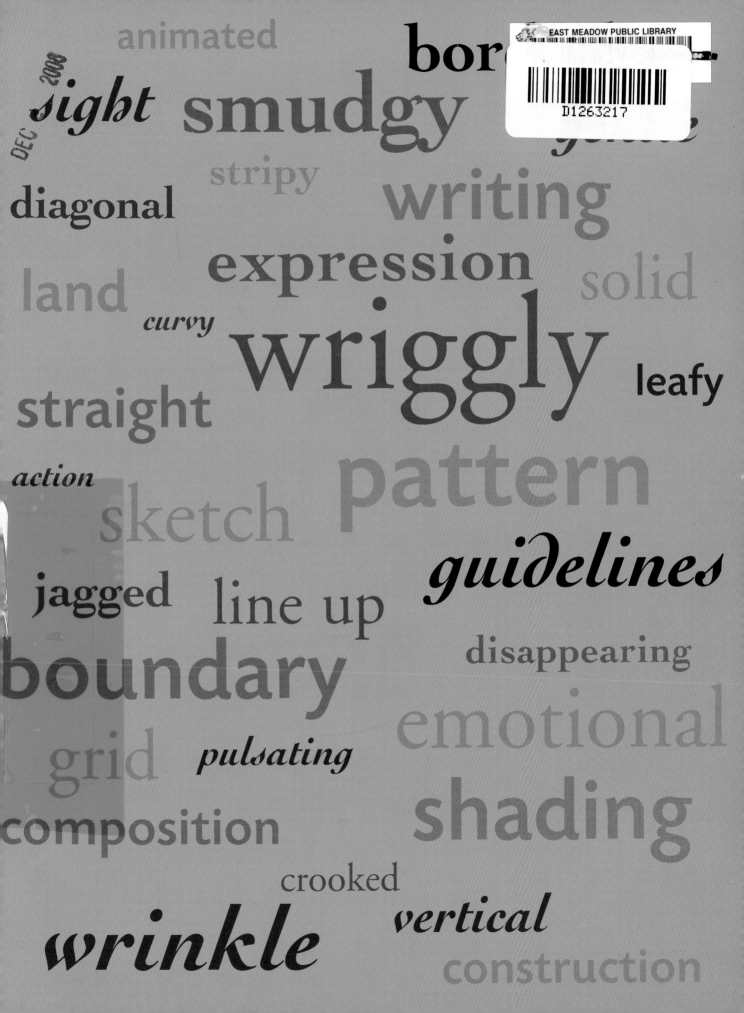

animated

bor

sight smudgy

stripy

diagonal writing

expression solid

land

curvy wriggly

leafy

straight

action pattern

sketch

guidelines

jagged line up

disappearing

boundary

emotional

grid pulsating shading

composition

crooked

vertical

wrinkle

construction

# LOOK!

## Drawing the Line in Art

*Gillian Wolfe*

F

FRANCES LINCOLN
CHILDREN'S BOOKS

For Valerie Austin, a dear family friend

PHOTOGRAPHIC ACKNOWLEDGMENTS

For permission to reproduce the works of art on the following pages and for supplying images, the Publishers would like to thank:

akg-images, London: front cover and 13 (© DACS 2008)
The Bridgeman Art Library/Private Collection: 20–21 (© Succession Picasso/DACS 2008)
The Bridgeman Art Library/Scottish National Gallery of Modern Art, Edinburgh: 14–15 (© ADAGP, Paris and DACS, London 2008)
© Trustees of the British Museum: 36–7 (PD Gg, 2.259)
© Photo CNAC/MNAM Dist. RMN - © Philippe Migeat: 26 (© Succession H Matisse/DACS 2008)
By permission of the Dulwich Picture Gallery, London: 4–5, 22, 23 and back cover
© David Hockney: 34–5
Collection Kröller-Müller Museum, Otterlo, The Netherlands: 38–9
The Metropolitan Museum of Art, Rogers Fund, 1918. (18.85.2): 11 (image © The Metropolitan Museum of Art)
Photograph © 2008 Museum of Fine Arts, Boston: 12 (Gift of Mr and Mrs Richard K. Weil. 59.574/© DACS 2008)
© National Gallery, London: 28–9
Philadelphia Museum of Art: 30–31 (The George W. Elkins Collection, 1924)
The Royal Collection © 2008 Her Majesty Queen Elizabeth II: 8–9
© Tate, London 2008: 18–19, 24–5
V&A Images/Victoria and Albert Museum: 16–17
© Virginia Museum of Fine Arts: 32–3 (Collection of Mr and Mrs Paul Mellon)

First published in Great Britain and in the USA in 2008
by Frances Lincoln Children's Books, 4 Torriano Mews,
Torriano Avenue, London NW5 2RZ

www.franceslincoln.com

British Library Cataloguing in Publication Data available on request

ISBN: 978-1-84507-824-9

Printed in China

1 3 5 7 9 8 6 4 2

# Contents

# Look – start with the line

One day the famous painter **Raphael was walking in the countryside.** He caught sight of a young mother with her two beautiful children. He longed to paint them at once but had left his painting materials behind. Instead he found some chalk and made a drawing on the bottom of a nearby wine barrel.

The drawing looked so lovely within a round shape that many other artists copied the idea of mother and child in a round frame, called a 'Tondo'.

Cave men drew pictures of the animals they hunted on their cave walls. They used burnt charcoal sticks, soot, grease and earth. **You can draw on anything** – paper, wood, fabric, leather, china, glass, mirror, metal, shells, stones, paving and walls. You can draw with icing on cakes or with a stick across the sand.

You can even draw on your own body with face paints!

Breathe on to a windowpane and when it steams up make a line drawing with your finger.

# *Look* – **sketch** lines

**Artists often make a sketch** before they begin painting. Look at this pencil sketch of Prince Krishna dancing. He wears earrings and jewels because he is so important. In India the god Krishna is worshipped by Hindus.

The artist pricked tiny holes around his sketch. He put the sketch over clean paper and dabbed black chalk over the holes. When the sketch was taken away the artist could see his design in lines of little black dots showing him where to paint. This is called a **cartoon** and is quite different from the funny cartoons you see today.

Where colour is added to the sketch you can see how the picture comes to life. What do you notice most – that amazing eye? The long snake-like lines of jet-black hair? All those jewels? Or the wonderful headdress?

Trace the head in this picture and prick holes around your outline. Put a sheet of paper underneath and dab powdered charcoal through the holes with a brush. Take away the tracing and join up the dots. This way you can repeat your design many times.

Rajput, Rajasthani School, *Head of Krishna: Cartoon for Mural Painting of the Ras Lila*

# *Look* – **doodle** lines

Paul Klee, *Tanzt Entsetzen (Danse Macabre)*

Some people call this sort of drawing **'taking a line for a walk'.** You could call it a wandering line, or perhaps a playful line, something you scrawl quickly without any planning.

To see how Paul Klee captures wild energetic movement, trace your finger along the single line of his dancing figure.

*Man with Big Mouth* has a wonderfully funny face. Just look at that massive chin, the sharp pointy nose, the little empty eyes and wriggly curls.

Can you see what happens every time one line crosses another? The artist has filled in each shape with a slightly different colour.

Make quick scribble drawings of faces or people moving. Do each one without taking your pencil off the paper until you've finished. Use jagged and curvy lines. Even better, try it with your eyes closed! Then make each part a different colour.

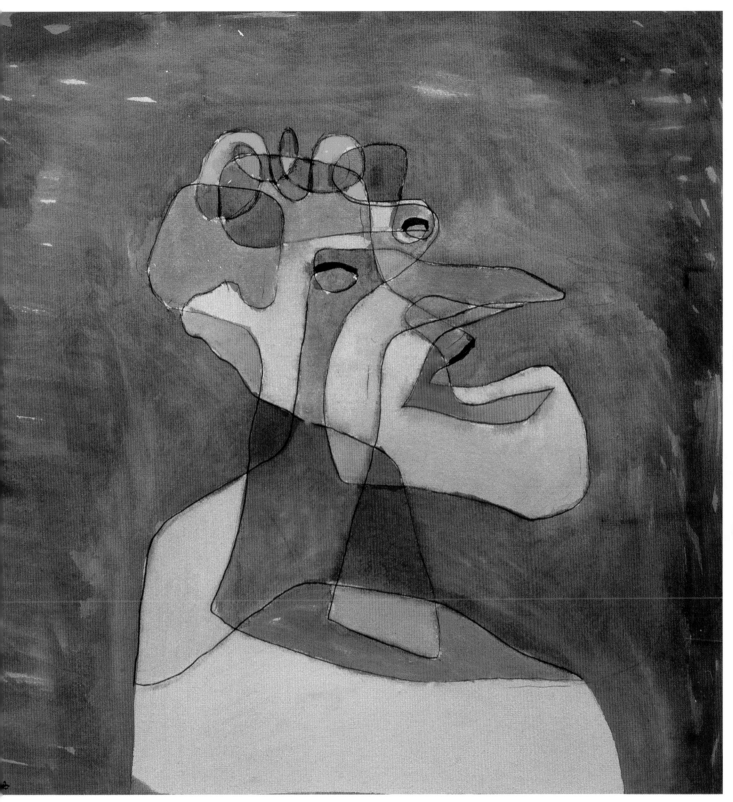

Paul Klee, *Man with Big Mouth*

# *Look* – **strong** lines

On this busy building site some of the builders are tired out and sit down for a rest. Others carry on fixing the metal frame of what might become a new house or factory.

Thick straight lines fill the whole picture and lead your eye right to the edges of the painting.

These clouds are not a bit fluffy – they have hard dark outlines to their curves. Even the curling rope and that very strange tree have solid edges.

The painting is full of **strength**, strong lines, strong colours and strong men with big hands.

Vertical lines stand upright, horizontal lines go straight across, diagonal lines lean over. Make a bold pattern using all these lines. Use strong colours. Thick felt tip pens are perfect for this.

Fernand Leger, *Study for The Constructors: The Team at Rest*

# *Look* – **delicate** lines

**Have you ever felt shy?** Can you remember a time when you were feeling small or worried about all the people or things going on around you?

Imagine what this country child is thinking as she gazes anxiously up at the famous artist painting her. Look at these delicate pencil lines, they hardly exist. Look at the thin paint – no more than coloured water washed over the girl from head to waist. A smudge of paint creates a shadow to make the girl's skirt stand out.

John Constable's **gentle drawing** is exactly right for this small child.

Make dots and jabs on your paper with sharp lines pressing really hard. Then see how gently you can draw, making lines that are almost invisible.

16

John Constable, *A Suffolk Child*

# *Look* – **symmetrical** lines

Two very grand looking women sit quite upright in bed. They look alike because they are sisters, probably twins. We know that the sisters were married on the same day and had babies at the same time.

On one half of a sheet of paper paint a face. While still wet quickly fold the painted half over and press down. You will have a symmetrical, repeated picture, a mirror image.

British School, 17th Century, *The Cholmondeley Ladies*

Everything in this painting is **balanced, even and regular**. The design is stiff and symmetrical. Lines and shapes are repeated, the women almost look like a mirror image of each other.

At first glance you might think the mothers are exactly the same. But the artist has not actually made them identical.

Look carefully at the two women and their babies. How many differences can you find?

Pablo Picasso, *A Cat Devouring a Bird*

# *Look* – **emotional** lines

### This cat is as fierce as any lion!

It follows the instinct of all wild cats to attack and kill its prey.

Picasso captures a ferocious scene. His massive cat has a monster-like body and fiendish face. Murderous fangs tear at the flesh of a dead bird.

Thick dark and light lines describe the cat's twisted face, alert ears and terrible teeth. Circles of black and white lines become menacing glaring eyes. Huge curling claws, heavily outlined in black, grasp the limp body of the bird.

The saying, *nature red in tooth and claw,* exactly fits this awful moment.

Draw your own furious or frightening face and make every line you use express terror or fear.

# *Look –*
# construction lines

Next time you cross a river, take a good look
at the bridge. These days there are amazing bridge designs,
but hundreds of years ago bridge-building was very difficult.

This painting shows a new bridge being built across the
River Thames. It was admired as the most beautiful wooden
arch in the world. The centre arch was high enough for a
boat with sails lowered to pass under. Sadly the bridge only
lasted 18 years before the wood rotted.

Peeter Neeffs, *Interior of a Gothic Church*

How do you know that some things are near to you and some far away in a painting? Artists are very clever at making you feel you can almost step inside a building like this.

This picture shows how lines can lead your eye into the distance. Shapes become smaller the further away they are, like these church pillars. The ones near you are made to look massive and those far away are so tiny you can hardly see them. Even the people are different sizes according to where they are in the church. This is called perspective.

Design your own wonderful bridge structure. You can make it beautiful, sleek, decorated and, of course, strong. Make your lines show the way it is constructed.

Canaletto, *Old Walton Bridge over the Thames*

# *Look* – **writing** lines

You know straight away that these boys
live in the city. Two Jewish boys stand on an
underground subway platform in New York.
Waiting for a train gives them a moment to read
a Hebrew book together.

Behind them the wall is completely covered
in scratched, scribbled and printed graffiti.
The messages are all jumbled up and become
an exciting pattern decorating a dull surface.
How many different names can you see
among the hundreds scrawled layer upon layer?
Artists often use words in their pictures.
Look at adverts and logos to see how clever
designers can be with letters.

Every letter is made with a line. Whole written
words are long *joined-up lines*
of letters. You take a line for a walk every time
you write your name.

Make a fun autograph picture. Ask
friends to write their names or messages
on a huge sheet of paper. Don't stop
until every bit is covered and you can
hardly see any spaces between words.

24

Bernard Perlin , *Orthodox Boys*

Bon                                                                    H. Matisse
                                                                        Juin 43

# *Look* –
# cut-out lines

## Have you tried cutting out paper shapes
and making them into a picture?

That is exactly what the artist Matisse did. When he was very old he was in a wheelchair and unable to carry on painting. Instead of giving up, he found a new way to make wonderful art. He had sheets of paper painted in the colours he chose. Without drawing anything first, he simply cut out the shapes he wanted and arranged them the way he liked.

Matisse had been a painter and sculptor. He once said that paper cut-outs allowed him to draw in colour. Even when a picture is made up entirely of shapes and colour, like this one, lines are powerful.

Can you see why Matisse called this picture *The Toboggan*?

Use patterned and plain papers – old magazines will do. Cut out shapes without drawing them first. Arrange them on a coloured background the way you want, then glue down your collage picture.

Henri Matisse, *The Toboggan, from the series entitled Jazz*

# *Look* – **land** lines

## What an astonishing landscape!

Lines of rock sweep your eye towards a fairytale city of pink stone in the distance. Lines of rock build up to craggy mountain peaks rising into the sky. Tiny plants, scurrying rabbits and a fallen tree-bridge over a green river all add to the oddness of the scene.

Angels watch as Jesus prays. His disciples have fallen asleep, not realising the danger. Round the bend comes Judas, another disciple. He brings soldiers along the long line of swirling road to arrest Jesus.

Even the figures are wrapped in **lines** of draped cloth. They look as stony as the rocks around them.

Mountains, fields, trees, rivers, roads, railways and towns can all be made with straight and swirling lines. Try it.

Andrea Mantegna, *The Agony in the Garden*

# *Look* – **dramatic** lines

Winslow Homer, *The Life Line*

**Shipwreck!** A woman is being rescued. She is completely exhausted and may be injured; we can see a glimpse of red on her knee.

Like a knight in shining armour a coastguard tries to save her life. Wind and rain lash at them but the man holds her tight.

Ferocious waves
threaten the pair
as the 'lifeline' pulls
them over freezing water.

This artist lived by the sea
and saw terrible events like this.

All the drama of the picture is
in the lifeline. It makes the scene full
of almost nail-biting suspense.

Lines mark out points of danger, like the edge of the platform at
the train station. Lines can show direction – like road markings.
Lines show expression on faces. Lines show age. Lines can be
dramatic.

Can these two helpless people reach safety?

Think of a hero like Robin Hood,
Superman or Harry Potter. Make up
a gripping story about a dangerous
adventure. Draw a final dramatic
rescue scene.

# *Look* – **leafy** lines

## When you look at trees and plants
you don't usually notice every single leaf.

Rousseau painted each leaf separately.
He loved strange exotic plants from
faraway countries; he said they
made him feel he was entering
a dream where he could be a
different person.

Although he never went to the
jungle himself, he shows us what
it might be like in forests where
tropical fruits and strange flowers
grow. But the beautiful jungle can be a
dangerous place. In this fight between an
Indian and a gorilla we wonder which will win. The
gorilla looks determined but the Indian has the weapon.

All around them are giant plants. Rows of sharp
spiky leaves seem to point at the small figures,
battling it out below a blood-red sun.

Henri Rousseau, *Tropical Landscape – An American Indian Struggling with an Ape*

Make a jungle picture full of fierce and strange creatures. Hide them among a mass of long leaves, tall stalks, exotic blossoms, wavy grasses and trees.

# *Look* – **stripy** lines

David Hockney, *Interior with Lamp*

Whoever lived in this room
# must have loved stripes!

Two enormous red-and-white striped sofas sit on a busy zigzag carpet.

Bookshelves are filled with strips of bookends. A fireplace is made of vertical and horizontal brick-line patterns. Lampshades are covered in line patterns. Find vases, twigs, flames, all are lines and stripes.

Pattern lines are in **everything** you see. Take a look around your own home and see how many you can find.

Make yourself a stripy, zigzag, swirly, wriggly pattern picture. When you make a lot of stripes close to each other they can sometimes make your eyes feel funny. Try it!

# *Look* – **solid** lines

Rembrandt's elephant has a big fat tummy, an enormous heavy head and legs like tree trunks. This is not an outline drawing.

What has Rembrandt done to make you know that this elephant is really solid? He used lines to make some parts of the elephant darker than others. This is called **shading**. Shading creates shadows. Shadows make things look rounded, as if they are solid.

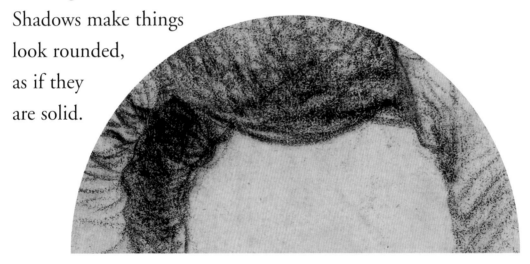

Although the elephant is a massive weight, Rembrandt used gentle almost smudgy lines to show the size and strength of this great beast. He also uses lines to show baggy skin folds on the back legs and neck.

Look at the people in the background. They are *not* shaded. Do they look **solid**?

Rembrandt, *An Elephant*

Draw an elephant in outline.
Then draw it again but now add
some shading and see the huge
difference it makes.

# *Look* – **texture** lines

A man travelling across the country was attacked by robbers. They stole his clothes and beat him up, leaving him for dead. A Jewish holy man came by but he walked past on the other side of the road. Next came a Levite, a man who helped in the Jewish Temple but he didn't stop either. Look carefully, and you will see them both in the distance. Then came a Samaritan who was filled with pity. He washed and bandaged the poor man.

This picture shows the moment when the Good Samaritan lifts the man on to his own mule.

Van Gogh has a special way of painting that you can always recognise. Every brush stroke is a line of thick paint.

Streams of swaying colour lines make the painting seem alive with movement.

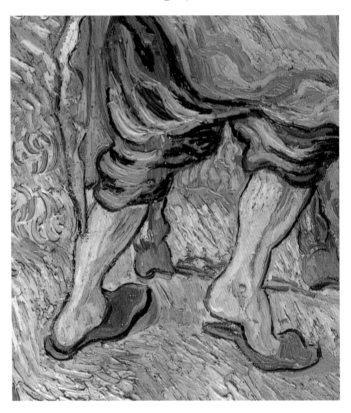

To paint with lines of texture like this you need to mix really creamy paint and almost dab it on in fat rows of colour.

Vincent van Gogh, *The Good Samaritan*

39

# *Look* it up

Here you can find out more about the art and artists in this book, including when the paintings were made, when the artists lived, and where you can see the paintings.

Pages 8–9
**Raphael's First Sketch of the 'Madonna della Sedia**, 1853
Johann Michael Wittmer (1802–80)
*The Royal Collection, London, UK*

Johann Wittmer was a German artist who trained as a goldsmith before studying to be a painter. He painted scenes from history and German religious art. Queen Victoria's husband, the German Prince, Albert, admired Wittmer's work and bought this painting to hang in a royal palace.

Pages 10–11
**Head of Krishna: Cartoon for a Mural**, c.1800
Attributed to Sahib Ram, Rajasthani School (c.1800)
*The Metropolitan Museum of Art, New York, USA*

Wall paintings, called murals, were once used to decorate grand buildings in India. One of the most talented artists employed for this work was the Muslim artist Sahib Ram. His masterpiece was a mural painting of Radha and Krishna dancing. Sadly most of these murals no longer exist.

Page 12
**Tanzt Entsetzen**, 1931
Paul Klee (1879–1940)
*Museum of Fine Arts, Boston, USA*

Page 13
**Man with Big Mouth**, 1930
Paul Klee (1879–1940)
*Paul Klee Foundation, Switzerland*

Paul Klee, a Swiss, was born into a musical family. His father was a music teacher, his mother a singer. Later he moved to Germany and married a pianist. His art has been described as 'Free Fantasy' and 'Poetic'. He was a brilliant teacher and taught at the famous Bauhaus art school. After visiting Tunisia in Africa, he experienced a whole new world of colour which ever afterwards influenced his art.

Page 14–15
**Study for 'The Constructors: The Team at Rest'**, 1950
Fernand Leger (1881–1955)
*The Scottish National Gallery of Modern Art, Edinburgh, UK*

Leger, a Frenchman, first studied architecture but after moving to Paris he was caught up in the exciting turmoil of the modern art world. He was greatly influenced by Picasso and Braque. His personal style of Cubism was based on mechanical shapes with shiny metallic surfaces and massive robot-like figures in strong colours.

Page 16–17
**A Suffolk Child**, 1835
John Constable (1776–1837)
*Victoria and Albert Museum, London, UK*

This famous English artist was not successful in his lifetime; he only sold 20 of his pictures although he achieved greater recognition in France. He had to paint portraits to make enough money to live but he preferred to work outdoors. He liked to paint watery landscapes with great windy skies. Many people know his painting *The Hay Wain*, a picture of the English countryside.

Pages 18–19
**The Cholmondeley Ladies**, c.1600–10
British School, 17th Century
*Tate Britain, London, UK*

Family group paintings like this were popular in the time of Queen Elizabeth the First and King James in England. We do not know anything about the artist and cannot even be certain about the name of the family. This pose has not been seen in any other painting. It is a mystery picture.

Page 20–21
**A Cat Devouring a Bird**, 1939
Pablo Picasso (1881–1973)
*Private Collection*

Picasso, a Spanish artist, was a child prodigy. During his long life he was never afraid to experiment with new ways of making art. Perhaps more than any other artist he changed forever the way we understand art. His powerful images sometimes seem distorted and disturbing. His work can now be seen in most modern art museums all over the world.

Page 22
**Old Walton Bridge over the Thames**, 1754
Canaletto (1697–1768)
*Dulwich Picture Gallery, London, UK*

Canaletto is perhaps best known for his intricate and richly decorated scenes of Venice. English tourists delighted in these views and eagerly bought his work. He came to England on and off over ten years and painted many English views. He was successful and popular.

Page 23
**Interior of a Gothic Church**, c.1630
Peeter Neeffs (1577–1661)
*Dulwich Picture Gallery, London, UK*

Peeter Neeffs specialised in paintings of buildings, especially the inside of churches. Sometimes he worked in partnership with other artists and his task was to paint the architectural parts of their pictures. He lived in Antwerp, now in Belgium, but in his day it was called The Netherlands.

Pages 24–25
**Orthodox Boys**, 1948
Bernard Perlin (born 1918)
*Tate Modern, London, UK*

Bernard Perlin was born in Virginia in the USA to Russian Jewish parents. After studying in New York and Poland he worked as a graphic artist and later as a teacher of art. With other American modernist painters he created powerfully realistic images of everyday American life.

Pages 26–27
**The Toboggan**, from the series entitled Jazz, 1946
Henri Matisse (1869–1954)
*National Museum of Modern Art, Paris, France*

Matisse began to study law and only came to painting when he was recovering from appendicitis – he described it as 'discovering a kind of paradise'. He became one of the leaders of modern painting and developed a highly decorative style using brilliant colours. When old and too ill to paint he developed a technique of cut-out designs in coloured paper.

Pages 28–29
**The Agony in the Garden**, c.1460
Andrea Mantegna (c.1431–1506)
*The National Gallery, London, UK*

Mantegna was the adopted son of a painter who was also an archaeologist. Mantegna himself became an expert on archaeology, so much so that it almost overshadowed his painting. His figures look solid, almost as if they were made of stone. He invented a clever way of making figures painted on a ceiling seem to float in space; this technique was copied by later artists.

Pages 30–31
**The Life Line**, 1884
Winslow Homer (1836–1910)
*Philadelphia Museum of Art, Philadelphia, USA*

Winslow Homer was influenced by his mother, a talented artist. His pictures of fishing and shooting scenes appealed to Americans but his real passion was painting the sea in all its moods. He settled in a remote beachside studio in Prout's Neck, Maine. Alongside the pounding waves he found all the drama he needed for his paintings.

Pages 32–33
**Tropical Landscape – An American Indian Struggling with an Ape**, 1910
Henri Rousseau (1844–1910)
*Virginia Museum of Fine Arts, Richmond, Virginia, USA*

Rousseau painted in his spare time while working for the French custom service. His self-taught style of painting is simple and direct. His strange dreamlike scenes are carefully painted in vivid colours. Picasso recognised Rousseau's unusual talent and this brought him to the public's attention.

Pages 34–35
**Interior with Lamp** , 2003
David Hockney (born 1937)

David Hockney is a famous English painter, a notable printmaker, a photographer and stage designer. He was the most popular British painter of the 20th century. He has a restless desire to experiment with new ideas and try new techniques. His overwhelming amount of artwork is wide ranging in style and astonishing variety.

Pages 36–37
**An Elephant**, c.1637
Rembrandt (1606–69)
*The British Museum, London, UK*

Rembrandt, the son of a Dutch miller, was a brilliant painter by the age of 22. At first he was wealthy and famous but did not manage money well and got into debt. He is a grand Old Master, one of the most famous painters of all time. His portraits are considered masterpieces.

Pages 38–39
**The Good Samaritan**, 1890
Vincent van Gogh (1853–1890)
*Kröller-Müller Museum, Otterlo, The Netherlands*

Van Gogh, a Dutch artist, is a modern master. He is famous both for his remarkable artistic talent and his sad life. He lived in dire poverty yet now his paintings are sought after the world over. His energetic, colourful and passionate style is immediately recognisable.

# Index

thick
shadow
pure
horizontal
clean
fine
doodle
delicate
dotty
broken
geometric
underline
scribble
traced
lined
groove
light
repeating
scar
angry
outlines
busy
skyline
technique
fussy
symmetrical
blotchy
lifeline
thin
furrow
vanishing
zigzag
wavy
printed